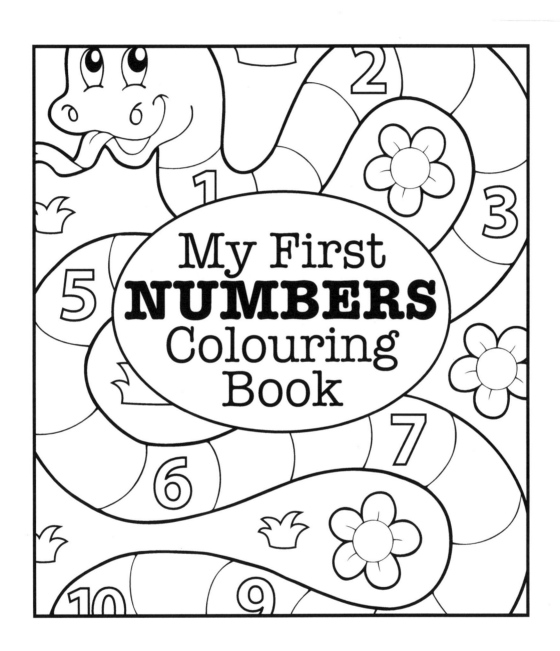

My First NUMBERS Colouring Book

Crazy Colouring For Kids

First published in 2016 by Kyle Craig Publishing

Copyright © 2016 Kyle Craig Publishing

Design: Elizabeth James, Julie Anson, Alison McNicol, Shutterstock, Inc.

ISBN: 978-1-78595-144-2

A CIP record for this book is available from the British Library.

A Kyle Craig Publication

www.kyle-craig.com

THREE

FIVE

6

SIX

NINE

TEN

One

Two

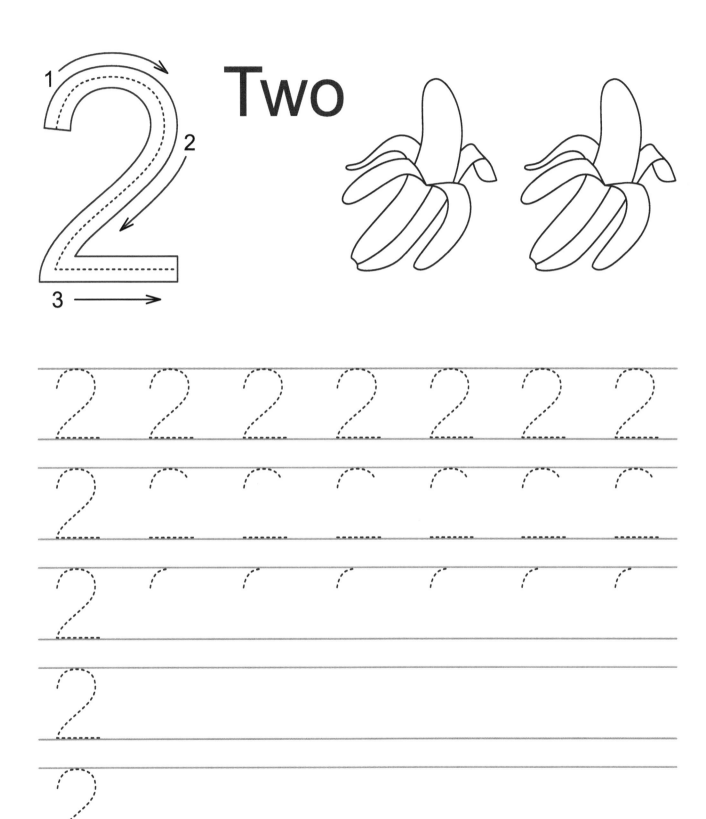

Three

Four

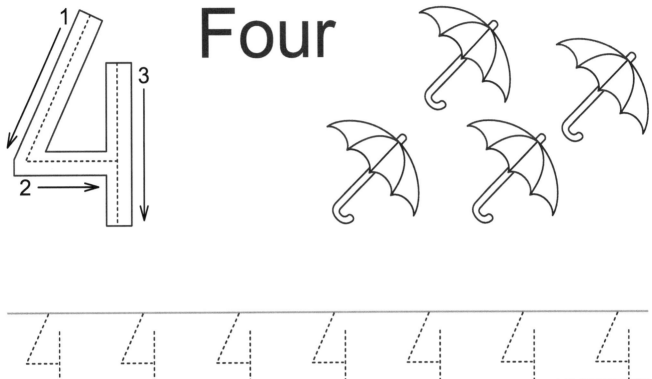

Five

Six

Seven

Eight

Nine

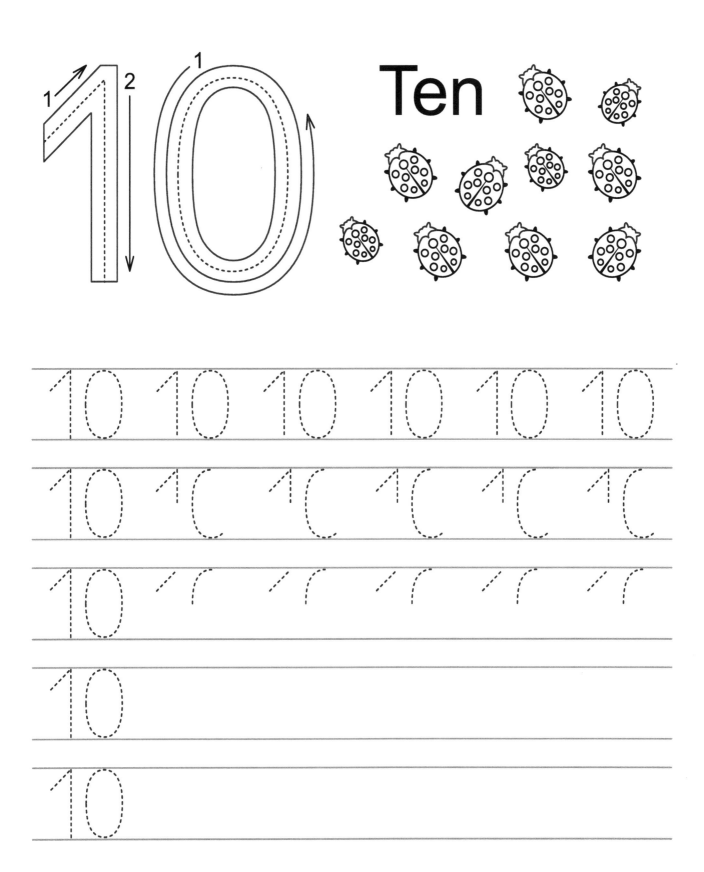

Ten

Let's COUNT

1	🍄	ONE
2	🍎🍎	TWO
3	🦆🦆🦆	THREE
4	🦋🦋🦋🦋	FOUR
5	⚽⚽⚽⚽⚽	FIVE
6	🧁🧁🧁🧁🧁🧁	SIX
7	🐟🐟🐟🐟🐟🐟🐟	SEVEN
8	🍓🍓🍓🍓🍓🍓🍓🍓	EIGHT
9	🌼🌼🌼🌼🌼🌼🌼🌼🌼	NINE
10	⭐⭐⭐⭐⭐⭐⭐⭐⭐⭐	TEN

Count and Match

Draw a line between each set of shapes
and the correct number

1 ▲▲▲▲▲▲

2 ♥♥♥♥♥♥♥♥

3 ■■

4 ⬤⬤⬤⬤⬤

5 ●●●●●●●●●●

6 ◆◆◆

7 ★★★★★★★★★★

8 ⬠

9 ✿✿✿✿✿✿✿✿

10 ✖✖✖✖

Counting Exercise

Join the groups which have the
equal numbers of pictures

Counting Exercise

Join the groups which have the equal numbers of dots

Printed in Great Britain
by Amazon